THE BRIGHT INVISIBLE

MICHAEL ROBINS

D1715785

saturnalia | BOOKS

Distributed by Independent Publishers Group
Chicago

Saturnalia Books
105 Woodside Rd.
Ardmore, PA 19003
info@saturnaliabooks.com

ISBN: 978-1-947817-43-2 (print), 978-1-947817-45-6 (ebook)
Library of Congress Control Number: 2022931370

Cover Image: Emily Dickinson herbarium specimen used with permission from Houghton Library at Harvard University.
    Dickinson, Emily, 1830-1886. Herbarium, circa 1839-1846.
    MS Am 1118.11 (seq. 19), Houghton Library

Cover and book design by Robin Vuchnich

Distributed by:
Independent Publishing Group
814 N. Franklin St.
Chicago, IL 60610
800-888-4741

Grateful acknowledgment is made to the editors of the following journals where versions of these poems first appeared: *American Poetry Review, Bateau, Bennington Review, Columbia Poetry Review, Court Green, descant, Ghost Proposal, RHINO, Trampoline,* and *Tupelo Quarterly.*

"The Other Way Around" draws its title from "A Song" by Joseph Brodsky; italicized passages in "On the Hundredth Birthday of Gwendolyn Brooks" are borrowed from "The Sundays of Satin-Legs Smith" by Gwendolyn Brooks and *A Life of Gwendolyn Brooks* by George Kent; "In Lovely Blue the Steeple Blossoms" appears in a fragment by Friedrich Hölderlin (translated by Richard Sieburth); "Though We Should Love Once More" is a variation on the phrase "though I should love again" from *Fatal Interview* by Edna St. Vincent Millay; "A Stone Endlessly in Flight" is borrowed from Book II of *Paterson* by William Carlos Williams.

The poem "An Elementary Survey of the Heavens" was written during a daily postcard exchange (February 2020) with Sara Wainscott. "Good News Will Come" was written during a postcard exchange (February 2018) with Noah Falck.

Contents

Oxalis violacea Hort.

Pinus quinquefolia L.

Clematis viorna Hort. &.

Orchis maculata Rich. &.

O Air

the clear, the soot-bearer, the unseen that rips
that kills and cures, that keeps
all that is empty filled, the bright invisible

into which we move like fingers into gloves
that coats our rolling home with the sweet softness
between grape and grape skin...

—James Schuyler

Against the Abysm of Time

It could've been an owl, some angel
or more likely a rather maudlin,
broken figurine, the pieces anyone

would sweep as my own mother tried,
played, I think, the thankful wife
there beneath the falls & into which,

unabashedly, I'd float when a crush
lay hold my hand that October,
possibly March & the foreseeables

longed for June, for the drawbridge
letting downstream a fleet of moments
done &, because to this very day

she slips farther away, heed my devils
while the children sleep or leave
our porch for the joy of a green hose

before one or maybe the other hollers,
cries, echoing again how I compare
flowers with grief & guesswork,

even the poet can't say whether smell
or a constellation helms the salmon
back for the shallows of her birth

so she can bury, fend the new eggs
before her body gives, weeks at most
& surely you've risen to that air

or the corner of Idaho & many miles
from your life, rubbing either eye
when you discover a brilliance slung

like an opal or alabaster across the sky,
lauded by those who didn't doubt
that a ball of ice circled the centuries

for them, thus welcomed both poison
& the finishing light ever so happy
to die, dwindle the backstreets

& canyons alike, the ageless hills
from which here & hereafter arrive,
commune, belt down the clear water

as conceivably they did along the shore
where I was born, began to crawl,
 swaggered in such grass or the insects

one after the other crossing the branch
& where, presumably, we'll return
to crowd & weigh our substance

among the birds & remember at last
which passage bears a willingness,
splits the world open, out of our lives.

A Debt Like Any Other

Under the medium, rare spell of a blue moon
without bringing to life your dress
& (almost) meeting the very challenge,

my short attentions rush & on the double
chatter like frozen logs. Figuratively,
darling, in which I'm ladybug doting sleeves

or else. The dog was like. The lake was like
many a mind likening the general drift
of a waterfall to the suggestion it's suitable

not for framing, fast as an errant crayon
never green, no aquamarine hung to the wall
& your midwinter thaw. Historically,

I return what remnants of sunrise outlast
spring, the real dozen beach towels
infrequently remembered, not quite treasure,

innate as crocus & dull. Your parcel calls to me,
my thingy, commingling awe & error
equally. A rhyme made apology, aroused

& treacherous too these stupefying sighs
ahh, my skull at night is thick, flickers slowly
before the tapped day settles & stitches

tomorrow's grass. Au revoir, my red-blooded
feet, chancing whatever flavors stick
& the sand that melts (always) to the heat.

The Day after Yesterday

I'm afraid his clockwork foolish, stray, mumbling
backwards & him, this one, not even a tadpole
cast around in shine, no bygones be bygones

nor artful way to describe the crowded weight
reddened, red on his mind its nest, its voice
speechless & frost while the neighborhood child

howls, heaps, & who from that curb ferries home
more fallen leaf than a loved, nearly living thing
& the boy, a tyke, better it him retreating oh

no one should finger the ash of winter jackets
blurred, waiting for the bus, the blink, the lyric
memory knows damn well not to straighten,

dumbstruck & swept with pigeon, whistle & clap
crossing flecks of sky from which a flurry begins
its drop, no fanfare rather whiskey to emblaze

such pastoral scenes under the gold, heady surface
tilted in a soup can or dirty glass, everything
sunlit to his lips & brain until a curious velocity

returns, this boy & his bottle a snowdrift buries,
their coupling flattened, dust, next to nothing
miles & cold, condensed over the latchless fence

where, indeed, now & then his rhythm stutters
& stumbles, steals the curtain whenever thought
inhabits gladness, together at the high window

abracadabra or, as if by chance, sometimes the sun
elbows the ordinary, archival cloud & my god
his key still opens that half-life, a charmless room

housing yet the meter he undresses, its mattress
& feather in the morning's catch, steady boy
landing anyhow between a whitewashed street

& wonder, knotted trees & the autumn echoing
boxcars, their freight a slice of southern valley
pictured on a postcard & him, this kid, moreover

bombed, cockeyed & split, no doubt confusing
recklessness with wild, the sidewalk with blitzed,
stacking a last ditch effort, no, not quite sex

& that not quite a blossom he pinches, this boy
unconnected like dots, pretending every kiss
his first, the hatchlings inside of which no animal

maddens, circles nor sinks a pillow by its teeth
but ripples, surfaces in time to startle the boy
fast from a story too often seen as frayed string,

pities laid bare & each one twining into a ball
tidy & toylike, painless to let go & what a flourish
to end it all, how convenient & excellent work

blowing out at will a match, closing the door
after a difficult impulse or weather, or the dead
shore of a lake where pleasure no longer lifts

any shirt, his own, the stone marked forgiveness
& where, to say it truthfully, if some decency
remains, he must be someone else, I know I was.

On the Wrong Walden Pond

Despite what we were told, notwithstanding
proper neglect for the writing on the wall,
no ordinary carrot tempts a rabbit to the crate
held open by a clumsy stick. In one account,

my correspondence patters like rain. In the other,
another year without you & coins like wishes
flood the streets. Last night, gone, some tramp
spilled my glass, pitched his barstool & asked,

Why aren't you making millions? Honestly,
I'd forgotten the sweater, that you'd even left
anything behind, & when I stretch its neck
over my head against the night's breath, I'm a fly

grooming the gate of my father's house. Ripe
for living, flitter & whiff, inhaled & hurled
like on a bender, they call such reflex common,
& my itch belated, burrowing a curious lawn.

The Other Way Around

More or less you measure the patterns of the scarf, pleated gray, & the flare of a wooden match as the vaporetto pushes out from the dock into the dark curves of water. No one steps in the same country twice, & so the noteworthy, Russian-born pilgrims have come to settle the cemetery of San Michele: Stravinsky floats next to Vera on a wide, flat stone; Diaghilev collects another gift of ballet shoes; & in the Protestant section, Joseph Brodsky lifts one of the many pens left at his grave to praise the haggard, wintry dust that blankets the cypress & frozen weeds, or to instead lob an insult at what remains in the nearby coffin of Ezra Pound. Memorize a poem & you'll ensure a civilization. Build a city on water & you test the impossible: doves into gulls into doves turning back between Leningrad & that apartment in Brooklyn Heights, its flight of stairs leading to the study where Brodsky passes a sheet of paper, a cigarette unsmoked, a book of Greek poems open on his desk.

On the Hundredth Birthday of Gwendolyn Brooks

With my son in the backseat, we weave an hour through midmorning
traffic & exit past warehouses, apartments, a public course for golfing.
We'd expected maybe a crowd, that string of admirers I measured (next
time) after Brooks read in what came to be the final months of her life. At
Lincoln Cemetery, alone, we circle her granite & recite a poem. *Life must
be aromatic*, she writes, but a girl tires of flowers, of cooking & sweeping
&, especially, the cold breath of a diagnosis: she left us almost immediately,
among family & friends & with a pen in her hand. Not yet three, my son asks
why these gifts for the poet who mirrors the day, whose etched likeness catches
even the wind of the nearby trees. Together, we make stories for the woody
cone, the candle & stone, trace the lucent shell a thousand miles back to the
sea. By the droves such favors will arrive & we will give them voice: *dropping
the mop, broom, soap, iron or carrot grater to write down a line, a word.*

Called Back

Before she crossed the quarter mile between the homestead & town cemetery, Emily Dickinson helped plan her own funeral. "Everything was white," one biography reports: white ribbons & textile handles, flannel for the lining ("five-sixths of a yard of Russian white") plus the robe that Susan, her sister-in-law, designed & in which the poet would be buried. According to further description, we should add the circumference of the flower garden to the distance traveled by the funeral party, then a single pass through the great barn that kept the family's horses. I've visited Emily's grave more than any other & while spring becomes summer in a snap, it was the beginning of the latter when, late one night & a dozen sheets to the wind, I hoped to marry past & present by launching my empty bottle toward what might've been a field of buttercup, where some bystander surely caught sight of six Irishmen (per Emily's instruction) carrying the poet's white casket.

In Lovely Blue the Steeple Blossoms

I mailed countless postcards from Tübingen during the earliest months
of my marriage. The poet Friedrich Hölderlin spent much of the
second half of his life there—writing under a pseudonym & plagued
by mental illness—before dying in 1843. I'd stop at his grave every few
weeks, suspecting already that my nuptials too would soon be buried.
I wandered the German streets as if it were my job, pausing now & then
to smoke a cigarette, eat the day's orange (my waistline shrank), or thumb
haphazardly *The Selected Poems of Frank O'Hara*, cover by Larry Rivers
& among the few books I'd packed for the fall & winter. I've since tried
Hölderlin, have mostly failed, but O'Hara surprises as he did even then.
For instance, in that grievous spell of my life, I remember looking up
from the page, following a curl or two on the surface of a nearby stream,
& believing there'd never come a better time to memorize a poem that
begins: "Hate is only one of many responses…"

Though We Should Love Once More

At the end of our marriage, as anyone should, we turned to the poets: a
cigarette with Bishop in Worcester; half an hour with Frost behind an old
white church; & lastly, in the hamlet of Austerlitz, a kind of reckoning at
the former blueberry farm where Edna St. Vincent Millay played the part
of the difficult wife & then, through that final year, the widow. We'd stood
up Millay before, paired guesswork with the AAA map & wandered the
public cemetery blind, drove East Hill Road to photograph the brackish
pool, the quiet house in which we swore the faint shadows of a dress. The
afternoon collapsed, spilled forward into weeks & months. One summer a
humid matrimony; the next, the last of our mid-twenties swerved toward
Steepletop. Past a clean placard & headlong down its trail, we pressed
an ear at last on Millay's resting stone. By then of course, in those New
England woods, there was no we. Alone & without so much as a word, I
asked of my teachers only everything.

A Stone Endlessly in Flight

—for WCW

Although no one expects the fever of last summer's fireflies, certain
hours ripple across the mouths of rivers—the Colorado & Mississippi,
the Susquehanna—& having clung to my paddle come what may, I pull
breathlessly north from Camden, revel the ground teeming with ghosts
of copper mines, of nervous horses, of the rabbit hunters &, among them
like President Truman, he who makes house calls, aims his flashlight,
examines the throat while a restless language hammers up from the
typewriters of Rutherford, forget not the boneyards of Lyndhurst & with
such pleasure for the perilous seasons in which a doctor set my arm, in
which a doctor made the hasty stitch, in which a doctor asked I follow
the shine, left & then right, easy now while outside the dogwood,
meadow, & milkweed begin once more their flowering, the harmless
mouse wrestles free, & this time that ancient lamp behind the clouds,
broad & timeless, waits for us where we left it.

Of Winter Sparrows

Come pointing yes, how common longing
dawdles, dense, wakes cumbersome
& my glances seek, they collide & need

such appetites we hush unto ourselves,
mid-page, under lampshade & often
worried, seldom a pinprick or the pricing

per inch of thread but in the white idea
expired, blind, hurrying that bicycle mine
toward enthusiasm yours. Our fenders

bang & momently bend, spokes blink the air
plausible & free. Christ, I'm culpable,
finger the holes in each knee to reenact

morning's ruthless scrubbing of the moon,
blue, incorrigible. By this conjured light
we're blush, aglow, more so a sparkle

swarming up the ladder until I'm slapped
gloveless, dropping out of February
buckets of the season's overdue muck,

leafy & poor, not felt nor fire but delicate,
fibrous, swiftly rare, my very thought
rung like an echo, like a midsummer joy.

The Twentieth Century

What fits near a matchstick. What hides
behind the bed. Douglas firs, a tower
winking on the hill & under them

some cherry tree, some Chesterfields,
our wild fingers & greener than the thorn.
For a dictionary a rose, & with a pocket

Kleenex from the funeral, the Kleenex
upon finding that each circle stalls,
moon & mother & joy. Yellow chins,

common salt to clothe the Irish daisy
& slug. What sweet tooth saves the vine.
What ache. What silver dollar in a drawer.

Someone Who Looked Just Like Me

When friends long dead confess a thing or two
what choice but heed their ghostly conceit
roving my lunchtime tray to the bored ceiling

tiny &, like yellow pencil, their directive hung
to right the narrow of windows ripe in crow,
lazy cows &, at the brim where a cemetery

ends & begins, you might imagine the urge
to ditch my grounds for being, southeasterly,
other days deny what spills dirt & a body

both, late tomatoes letting go & charged down
like fire between your town & the heavens,
your child's fright & another while I'm caught

stuttered (oblivion ha!) halfway out the yard
& difficult, startled by the headless rabbit
wet on the paving stone, salient patchwork

nearly intact & with its fold, with the branches
bare & those in bloom, I mark no phoenix
off the sludge but (because scaffolds swerve

my eyes from the sidewalk gum to that swift,
steady washing of marble) my coordinates
shift, stumble the watermelon rind & alone

toward seed, fatal where the feline's tongue
gladdens the fur of her right leg, then her left
routine as tending a grave, expecting some

company yet & furthermore with inside jokes,
punch-lines for every synapse but the one
counting back from ten, never quite getting

joy, its heart snaillike & down the middle
until snapped when my only daughter shouts
she's so angry she could hit a thousand cats,

raindrops that look to her like turned off lights
& I hear spit in the empire of crude trucks,
common flies swept in the painting of a face

then a fence, I hear December with the dog
blind in her garden, hear a buckling door
& hear the softened fruit, hear furrow & hear

crosswind while my mind builds this father
scaling the clouds for a child, that height
sudden & from which worry fits the thimble,

love & love-me-not blown like dandelion heads
between what's possible & where I believe
collecting rock delivers no safety from the sea,

such breadth & airlessness, lamps overturned
then sunk beneath the crests, beyond deep
& suggesting my friends own less than water

& so, to their curious visits, I reply with thanks,
ask we pass together the gates into a meadow
or the dappled thought of grass that anchors

these green now purple dogwoods, inviting
our measure to the stranger who knelt, cradled
not some lonely tree but went & planted two.

In Praise of the Sleepless Plum

The fleas overstay, work midnight to dawn
where I close my eyes & become that boy
posing in spring a candy cigarette. I remember
waterlines, the way of starfish down pilings
like a cheekbone pale in the deep. Thresholds
scrape my lung, then cart a turn of mercy
neither offered nor received. Every skin now
struts its feather, lilies, the westward arrow
to the ends of history marking both alley truck
& tenure of a child's bear wired on its grill,
these totems that sway my throes, & my love.

In Lieu of Flowers

—for Huda Al-Jaburi

She dreams beneath the washed-out trees
& the other, tell me again of his heart
cornered like a rat when the sliver moon

rises early, delights at last the rabid dog
while we rewind our clocks against reason
so even the hour of a wrist orbits twice

those dozen shades broken & yellowed,
scattering their heat & off to an underbelly
before we buckle or straightaway gather

what's happened for in the instant we blink
our neighbor won't, & if rang the bell
it dropped inside the crosshairs, & if ever

floated a pitcher to bear her soul like water
we did not see it but instead the vestige
almost nestled & drowsy with snow,

flurry of jewels we've known lovingly cut,
descending, sweeping the lit windows
& they charm the eye, increasingly please

until the greyhound of time remembers
every branch must lay down its green,
demands of our labor to say the unsayable,

how we wanted to believe our neighbor
asleep, the sky an ordinary kind, then swore
to forget not the moon & her threshold

coupled steady in the grass, but that other
whose sick & godless sound we leave
deserving to die &, so with him, it does.

An Elementary Survey of the Heavens

—for Sara Wainscott

I

January sentenced & without a color
by her peers. Like loitering. Like time
taken from the cat's meow & along
comes dawn of sensible intentions why,
generally I wouldn't but what's the big idea
or deal. Before & after. The hundredth
balloon out of Germany where we cannot
easily remember the names of flowers
anyway. Like January leapt unauthorized
& so they cut the power to the tracks

II

readily as bikini string & later those stars
reclined, made a dark spectacle. Us & them
both, & summer still comes like my girl
for a cough drop in the middle of the night:
we will have our sunglasses, we will surrender
several pair to appease the waves. A dream
as much as anything, the slow child wants to see
window dressings undressing &, northbound
instead of south, suppose we'll never fish
beside our fathers again. Well, that's enough

III

of the days stitched in the lining of a week,
feathers on arrows sing by way of wishes
across the picnic spread. With bookish
intention, what a far-fetching candle
setting the patent office aflame. I admit
this trying to eschew the now, clause
upon clause & for some eighty-five years
you'll be becoming, conceivably a Luddite
while clerks wear holes in their shirts,
chitchat over money, crowd one another

IV

out from the busy parking lots & eking back
anew, narrow spaces & the memories idle
like, like engines & like impatiens align,
headfirst & up. Such odds & ends can strew
my breakfast everywhere, save for the coffee
heavy with honey on the rim. As ever,
I await a sentence from the postal carrier,
language no more imposing here than a pebble
out in the flowerbed, which in turn happily
closes each of its eyes. It happily shrinks

V

overnight, beneath the first frost of autumn
& by winter the abusive, alliterative bird
tears the dream in half. I might've said
midstream, little plateaus the dashes
& at times the printed letters make. I like
lulls as good as anyone & only a century ago,
amidst women airing handkerchiefs, the talkies
were all the rage. Those arrows of the past
didn't plan to upstage our cosmic lunch:
they're funny in that way, not ha-ha funny

VI

& writing you into these mornings I'm afraid
I neglect the moon. Taking what was, what
five o'clock or the quarter till. Taking the ruler
from the Dollar General, separated anxiety
or taking clean the falling trees, how they sound
if no one's there to post it. In a moment
I split my chin, split my chin, again my chin
to the hovering, surgical light. Downstairs,
delightful as sleeping pills, take the kids,
mine or yours. It's me who puts them there

VII

elbows right, left, & nudging to the front
as they often do. Chances of weather
overnight, the likely news of quarantine
& please, cover your mouth. Fi & fo,
fum & fee, them doctors cut us piecemeal:
"toe bone collected from the foot bone"
etcetera. As if our mothers will even care
after no more salt, no kick of postcards
endorsing the Floridian courthouses
(breathless!) or an astronaut's costume

VIII

certified, authentic with powder-like dust
& nonetheless dazzled, brighter than the cusp
between decades. We used to say parasol,
find them strange nowadays in the sun-filled
streets when the long afternoons reduce,
their prices slashed & done for in rigmarole,
too soon & two-second rules. Schoolboys
learn the leaves & licorice root, cherry bombs
over the brink of gravel pits. It's January,
March or even April. It's 1953 or otherwise

IX

your satisfaction guaranteed. Grown in a moist,
rich soil &, for one weekend only, it's where
I held the rifle & fired. Friend of a friend's
& for you I'll spare a catalogue of foolishness,
benefits of certain doubts & those bedrooms
I considered home. By the fourth or fifth
cup, I'm my own wobbly fall in a very
public thorn. High, this wine that either
doubles a man or kills him. I'd better luck
holding back the tide than emerging unscathed

X

while ironing, some cleaning, some before
thoughts of a birthday starting up like the cry
when the cat wants in. Almost forty-four,
having never spent an hour in jail, I've met
many a sentence only to find my shovel
by the boots & covered in the snow
just near the door. There's a new rug
advertising blues in our open living room
&, after a shortcut by the practice fields,
my sense of a somersault slows down at once

XI

for the crowd will abandon all braininess
upon discovering the patches of grass
underneath, the glad stones that bottom
icy streams. The kids on the telephones yell,
"Sell! Sell! Sell!" & view suspicious stamps
that pay the way for a dispatch or valentine
or late payment in the mail. I hereby recollect
ducking in a local pharmacy for Reese's,
browsing one, maybe two thousand books
& making space for them anew on my shelves

XII

like clearings for honest statues. In May,
June or July we spy the ghosts of last summer
tattered & torn where the hornets buzzed,
bodies like electric hammers in a nest
abandoned, empty for good. The scene
spills minor nudity &, therefore, it lingers
like an after-party. I'll pony up for drinks,
at best a well-worn frequency, literally
& no bridge close enough to toss a dagger,
laughter, the weight of a human form

XIII

& despite her clean alibi, here the weather
buries paddleboats & a tandem bicycle,
slaps inches onto the shore. It's how
they traveled in the day, backpedaled
up & down the aisles of the general store,
strollers around the block & everyone
every which way. As for the clouds,
still they frame the same moon & stars
& who can tell if it's the heart or a loose
thread of the red scarf floating like air

XIV

yes, the old chicken-or-egg commotions
where mowers scatter just enough twilight
to sleep the cold season through. Maybe
you'll share with me the consequence
for dreaming of deep meadows, perchance
it'll meet us before these months go mum
& delivers the child's dog that needs
more stuffing. Momentum cannot stop,
will not stall, & truth be told I might've
married a shuttering, a Christmas card

XV

painstakingly threaded, finely glued, hinged
within a bottle. Longing to glisten, to transfer
songs best suited for a Saturday or Sunday,
one quarter of the notes lost in leaping
feetfirst among the fans & leafy fluttering
like letters from Chicago Furnace or WTTW:
Dear Valued Customer… At most I'll brag
these houses I've made for words, the would-be,
could-be visitor who passes my lampposts
& stairs. Better, I think, my days build a pier

XVI

from which to drop a coin, lower my can,
bacon hand over hand on a string. From which
planet Earth, bewildered & middle-aged,
will try any innovative ruse. I've my stacks
& shares of apartments too, greater in number
than my exes who include a dance, a sack,
liars & mischiefs. The trick is to have a trick
like sleeping while streaming, an elbow
delivered this instant. My mnemonic devices
graze in a country unsuitable for walking

XVII

& so we catch the train or even the next one,
boxes in the shape of greasy triangles cast
about the platform. The world slurs "no duh,"
hurries &, when we're in it, I seize a glove
smaller than my own. I lead it between
bakery & bookshop, shoe store & sundown
& around a puddled slush, the awakened,
working stink from the week. In full,
martial night, now's the time for wonder,
to love my girl when she names a blazing star

XVIII

with whatever phrase or half-remembered
spectacle, similarly pulling the long way
outward & gone. Last night's dream
beds amid other sleepers & for my maker
I press On, scroll today's bankruptcies
while awaiting that first cup. Later,
offering grounds & a very good Tuesday
down for the compost, I'll think twice
& nearly dead of the joy inside a box:
hunger fed, nerve alone sensing my light

XIX

behind which the rooftop or shadowy fence
melts to the sky while a bowtie trails
its yellow kite. So say I grew from there,
surprised myself with dashing for a bus
or elevator. That's a lie. My sniffling
slips in one year & out another, worries
maybe just a hair on the tip of the tongue,
ampersand & ampersand playing keys,
pumping the pedals. Feelings right there
& like Indiana traced in the fold of a curtain

XX

or the contrails freezing the blue flyway,
those whistles dialed to eleven. Daily,
nonstop migrations sweep Emily Dickinson
right from her thrilling grave. Swelling
side to side, colorful splashes & size
short-lasting in the washing basin. Well,
August & September oughta reconcile
like a Sunday organist & the organ donor,
moth-eaten signals between my house
& occasional home. Cool reckonings

XXI

look up their meaning & first known use
such as a feather, wing, or fin. Pick a crayon
& tell me about your day. We go white,
gray really, & rush to each other's secrets
should we fall. Counting carbs & the like
against the fiber, rain, & the local Girl Scouts
back ringing our bells. A tramp of hours
visit every neighborhood. We mustn't
walk too fast, elsewhere these possibilities
compulsory like a census, free of punctuations

XXII

& opposing the bellflowers. A paint or two
placeholding proper shades. With blood
from a cut from a paper that was a Thursday,
constant sorrow & so on. This parting
succumbs to gravity, sits unwell & swears,
couplets becoming three in the birdbath
turning muck under the sun. Guessing
I should stretch before switching seasons
or the porchlight out. The blue betta
veracious & flaring wide inside his tank

XXIII

when I lean close, consider how the gears
shift into the weekend arousing spring:
"It's been too long," she says. Silver change
between the bricks, numismatic as they come
& why not a cool beer. I wanted an ocean
but settled on a short stroll among the statues
then aisles of endless stuff. More & more I think
I've reached the imaginary emergency brake
as we imaginarily roll backwards, maybe a cable
frayed & no connection. Brutal, just brutal

XXIV

for we hear before we suffer what's trapped
itself in the ductwork & let the combustion
doze through the night. My own address
gathered by the height of a tree, lefty loosey
& casted spells like the ship, or butterflies
lifted off the lampshade, or cherry blossoms
seized with the curbside flood. I've read
our land right here is the lake bottom's land,
traffic about what you'd expect. Diving
ducks & destiny. The sandbars serving tea

XXV

to the marram grass & go figure: takes more
than a goldbrick to fool anyone. Why not force
two sticks like their cousins, scrawny legs
that scissor behind the swimmer a dozen feet
from the seawall. Or instead the icepack
or try the heating pad. Try a citizen's arrest
& spotting the decade-old proof of a pencil lead
almost breaking the skin. I've had it to here,
Cleverness. Under my father's binoculars,
I cannot say I was made from a famous comet

XXVI

or cupid, chicken scratch along the margins
&, tinctures later, I holed my one true parachute
during launch. Places of deep mud or mire,
I've feigned a natural passage, replaced
bulbs & cleared pathways inside then out
where workers come in time. For the snow
sometimes a broom will equal any garden tool,
hustling the steps for kisses between now
& October. Like hauling the floats & sinkers
together. Sacked mushrooms. A net of potatoes

XXVII

gently down the alley &, nope, domesticity
impresses nobody. With mouths to feed
every half hour, suppose there's my chance
(wild-eyed in the sidecar) for it's true
some horse left me with a New England
slice of these United States. Such brilliance
wrestling free, cooking again the days
medium rare. What a meal in a nutshell:
November, December, the word "pioneer"
attached by itself in the obituary section

XXVIII

& representing courage, strength of mind
what have you. Thereafter the banter
winding, weeping, whittled like perfect
rods twirling dessert on the fire. Remember
to wash well when you've handled a nail
uncovered in the unflowering bed. Remember
afternoons that veered into the liquor supply,
retreated for the fictional touch or colors
clustered in shrubs. I'm out of practice
replying Goodbye, our final missives ready

XXIX

before the month shutters its windows, closes
shop for new work waiting, nuts or bolts
we cannot budge, not today. Another beast
& other flourishes when the night relents,
spent condominiums to the sky. I tried
sailing first a box of records across the sea
& knew the water cold. The gall of it all,
even the rusted hulk of a car where a cliffside
meets the beach. That is how I'll miss you,
each boot unknotted after I've locked the door

XXX

& at last, a curiosity or plain nostalgia turns
back to the opening pages. See here the steamer
makes port after all, & our manner keeps
like a widowed mitten left to the crosswalks,
property of garages & lots & the better day
tuning my watch to the river. Morning,
noon & night, overhead the same swelling
& since we count our senses one through five,
let's fly & hurry the arrows from our lips,
pin our ears between the trees &, yes, soon.

Outer Banks

Like a bottle in sand or the scoop of a pelican
not terrible in the least but diving for what fish
float near &, when from the darkness I wake

or await a sign or grow tempted to give over
my life to the ghost crabs, our star like a red whale
punctures into the singular flower of the world

& I climb up tipsy through the vanishing gauze,
ocean flared & erasing my ten toes, shoulders
less fluorescent or more the beach umbrella

anchored in photographs as though every August
we ever tried, remaking the ring of its story
when turns of an outboard become the mower

& the thrum of the sprinkler's *shhhtik-tik-tik*
top the riptide & shipwreck, or maybe a trowel
tossed in the garden plot fetches & tips the sun

until, out from the marram grass, your hands
like butterflies rest their spell on my knee
& I'm moored into the crook of your elbow,

hungry as a black-headed gull for the nautilus
dressed in weed, buckets to float my boat
or splash & tease down both our bare waistlines

while the shiver suggests, reaches & revels
even the depth that slips from shore, syllables
rounding a tongue like salt & the next summer

ripples between a shoal of minnows & the waves
steadfast, one after one, faithful unto the last
where we sink or swim that good morning sea.

Rite of Spring

With apology & with the thrust. Where the shovel dropped & in the hole of sufficient depth that my shoulders dug. Each rotation connecting the arm, the arm extending my hand while the wiring of its flexion calls back (always back) to the brain. With the brain suspended from the heart. With the song subtracted from its feathers. With the tremor & then without.

On Negative Capability

In a month of Sundays, which is to say
beneath the sheets alone, awoken,
heeding the sickly world that at times

still finds a grace note, upholds the loam
& its sudden bouquet from the rain
after weeks without. You cannot tell

if the stairs merely shrug or bid the work
waiting to be done, whether dawn
untucks your sleep to carry out the dog,

mix the wet & dry as she moves by smell
near the bowl, or if her soft collisions
have come to the field of memory

every which way sprung with mustard
& muskrat & tennis balls. In other words
be the shelter akin to a silver maple,

never the chorus that prefers applause,
goes dull, forsaken as the on-again
off again downpour. Like those birds

who wobble, roll their necks side to side
& mate for life, you weigh each day
with the promise claiming half the bed,

suspect what probability renders the night
heavy & bricklike, or in the morning
holds the cherry blossoms to their trees

despite everything. Although you know
even children suffer blue monotones,
you must deliver all fact & reason

staring out the shadows of a nearby home,
one which this strange, fickle century
floods & hurries anyhow to the ground.

Bewilderedness

Out of tangles, scrap & braided grass, I've given up
this simple raft, my raggedy shirt to the blind,
blinking ships. Not so dramatic as all that
for the town of Detroit lands squarely in Oregon
& summer boys troll its lake, a bounty I'd say
except I couldn't drop a knee to bludgeon my catch,
feverish in the foot of the boat. It's what I dub
my hard, habit-forming cowardice. Stubborn time,
might kindness shake your dreadful meaning
& hang again the map that boasts the pearl
of a plainspoken mirror. Often I render the dead,
seldom a master who, against the shoreline,
demands we abandon desire, perennial blossom
that leads a fish upstream then back again to the sea.

Poem for the End of Winter

Now that you've set down your pen, whatever
waits next on the bullheaded list of To Do,
now & by no accident after a season ruptured

you clear the vines to reveal a threshold, frost
wept around the stones & shortly, as the daffodils
raise their arms, you'll try from the old depths

your bare tune & say as though for the first time
I can't believe she's gone or Father, I love you
or I'm sorry it happened at all & now I know

how I was wrong. Perhaps, despite the weather
& festered hope, there opens this other room
when you understood there'd be zero left,

no capacity in the chest that trembles afraid,
neither for the art of losing tightened & strained
unto itself, smaller, seemingly without air

to bear the frightful sail of your breath. Gently,
this breeze nonetheless & here now drifting
between strangers up early walking their dogs,

sleepy nods or rasping hello beneath the cold
because our eyes, those stalled & those put out,
they mirror our marrow, the motley shapes

through which we sometimes imagine the soul
like a church bell swung & beheld. In ache,
hesitation, our hearts ring true & more precise

than the careful, boring, dumbfounded words
that stow the memory & those that send you
headlong into a new life. You count the flowers,

point to spring &, at the trailhead of the world,
surrender your chair, a tired scarf like a rag
left for the scrap & heap of such consequence

no bigger than the sliver, a comma, no bigger
than the tail of that comma, no bigger than seed
spun by the spider or the syllables of a name

whispered in your ear, no bigger than a promise
for the mending becomes us, owns no watch
while the days invisibly collect behind the snag

& broken branch & which, maybe tomorrow
or a month thereafter, inch by inch begin to spill,
let go, release. So it is we come to the cool,

tall & unfolding trees noted for such patience
& the birds not those of elegies but their missives
unannounced, a swell likewise calling home,

gathering from the ground every last snowdrop
&, with due respect, asks only that we know
our regret, return to the present hour & choose

differently, to notice how the darkest shadows
ease toward green &, by a similar tenderness,
bask in the bounty that follows, a warmth

you haven't yet forgotten. Like fingers of light
that circle & lull your shoulder into its hold
& once more, this minute, now again step into it.

Against Long Island

Over a river sober & through our screens
we go, stomaching trees & their cuts
soon bracing a home. It means less
than pickled fanfare, felt in pictures

fooling my love around with the grace to be
born & (scrolling variously as possible)
call it a life. Once, the advice of fathers
standing like a mailbox as we drove away.

The satellites nod, route a faster course
past the urge to idle long at the fence
& seed a plot or two toward our younger,
more vulnerable years. What jubilee

spying bluebells & the daffodils ballooning
for me, only me, forever each for me
when, if anything, the bed in my eye
baffles & thins, blows as it must & quits.

During the Great Hummingbird Wars

—for David Berman

Like a snake, the whatnot cool of twenty
sheds its charm &, at the age of forty,
taking by storm the continental breakfast,

you whistle a tune until the notes flatten
like a Henry F. Phillips screw. Against
such early lights, lacking prayer or science

you merely trust enough that the towel,
rheumatic from its rack to the floor, makes
mountains upon which the candle left

hanging inside your head might beckon
whichever way leads to elation. Like sand,
so are the piles of Maryland everywhere

& today the eggs, having more or less peeled
themselves, would much rather fester,
soften & squat among the half-eaten toast

than not be chosen at all. For a dull word
played nice & buttering up the weather,
another races kerosene to the whitened heat,

awakens a man who happily slices & flays
kindheartedness, those split heirlooms
working magic from the vines or where,

wah-wah, the shiver of a trombone yawns
& slides. Further seismic, modern facts
include the lily, how clouds beyond number

rear elephants &, beneath what's surely
becoming an otherwise splendid afternoon,
you oblige a starless frequency to assume

your brace position, fray the very oxygen
when it fumbles the hose of its mask,
& rush your confessions for the faceless,

dissolving sky. While a speck of donkey
bearing walnuts over the Yunnan Province
rings true, back inside the hotel lobby

nervous guests pin flowers to their blouses
& soak what frills call a Weekly Saver
home. You prefer sipping the thin coffee,

daring the bait & switch of the story line
other than the one that waves goodbye,
lowers a bird into the coalmine of your life

& deepens for you the prayers of the boy
who more, more lately trips the rope
skipping inside your chest. Who can guess

whether that child will survive without you,
no gambit passed down the family tree
except the hours bent on a second & third

bowl of mush. Close to twenty-two months,
gestation for African elephants is nearly
twice the tenure of the donkey & all things

merit their sway: the fish & netted moon,
seedlings at the bottom of a paper cup,
cock-a-doodle-doo & the glowing porch

that promises to bathe our common dread
softer than a feather, a newborn's wrist
& the ancient, white fields of your own bed.

The Bright Invisible

Early such darkness, these oncoming nights
& sure, I'm dull & even slow to concede
how mornings make equal, swerving measures
there between those foremost shadows
along the fence, amid the chickens & nerve,
sheep & their indifference to any pair of fools
helpless in love, who visit through the cold,
shortened, everyday hours like you & me
until, oh yes, we take the prairie like pioneers,
plumb the woods with a memory of wildflowers
& the skinny, skinny leaves released as purely
as the dead houses that will, come spring,
vanish in fits of a blossomed green & the singular
awakening in which we kiss, merely a blink
like the hurried bird across the canvas of light
& afterwards, in that heave, our mothers
swell, our own fathers relish again in the flesh
& without, I'm told, any timeline for grief
or retrieving their clothes among the fallen trees
where we sit together, feed the river like so,
dare to welcome the center of this bare,
wild kingdom, the brisk & wondrous possibility
when we lean into the sun, close our eyes
& describe for each other what colors appear.

Good News Will Come

—for Noah Falck

Suppose out the window & reckon
not the swept fields nor them squirrels
dared & defying electricity, but a stupefied
lark of the sea. Suppose in its meadow

you've dove blue & I've yet to fall
or, another way, I'm the old complaint
ready to fetch a greenhorn in the bar,
its only customer. That isn't dawn

chewing this middle curtain, stuttered
forth as though to hollow some egg
before cursing backwards, cutting short
her path to another shore. I've oft imagined

such archaic vernacular, the multitudes
out of myrrh like any string of horses
& their swimming. Suppose you believed
I'd picture a quarry merely to fix a lake

above the framework of a man. Well,
even for the life of my child I cannot stop
our cursive from drying, two fingers
vanished off a hand, then the next three

where once more the season emerges
hammy, flaunts the loosened chain
clean into the air. That fissure opens
like a parlor trick, double, doubled twice

when filed in our eye, plainspoken light
beyond the low-lying gasp of the volunteer
who joins the fray & from pleasure,
need, out of momentum cedes the plains

wheeling onward. Now a tea towel,
now a cheek, now in the house a doctor
otherwise this long story long. I splash
water for the color we understood,

our thin, fainted footprints stacking up
each time you mention a yellow star,
oh how pyramids cross their arms whatever
& smear, cancelled, a slight stationary

torn at the fold. Instead of fold say plot
& where a thinker goes when you say
summer. Like the ordinary fireflies
we counted six seven eight & the dead

hid, stay hidden past midnight after we load
our pockets, return to fluid obedience
over the shallow, self-medicating lawns,
their Adirondack chairs. The tourists

come & crowd a rectangle paddock
planted in a rectangle park. One of us
chomps clover, inches to the baby grand
&, apropos of nothing, aligns his wrists

before they buckle like gods. Thou art
pitied, pitiful, despite its very sound
rarely the twain together. A promise
knots a sheet to the flowerbed & our father

shrinks to the size of a puddle, worried,
with no relief as if it were you or me
leaning outside the door, all nonchalance
booted for war. Suppose now a breeze

tips the contents of your glass, now
memory, predawn, & the search party
dissolves. For the love of the river
we're bound, ferried, reciting often

how in the mouth of a drainpipe the cat
better tends her litter. Each echo here
resembles bone, a figment versus fragment
faraway & nigh, my sightedness dextrous

& sinister, darling & vinegar, nearly
sprung. By the light of a teenaged decade,
we take a breath, tuck it for the wallet
left beside a winter pond. Your tiny boat

sleeps crooked, its anchor scraped down
around the boy's ankle. A month slips
speechless, then surrenders a letter
addressed in your own scrawl. One

& one accumulate behind us like snow,
higher than a mind can stretch the grass
toward corners we call home. For my part,
I'm afraid that sickness (happy rambler)

climbs again the step, from both its feet
wipes the world & rings the bell. The day
sails its pages &, turning in the rear seat,
looks but once. Tomorrow says soon,

please don't go, swears I'll be different
& love a little more. I've seen the wiring,
seen rain as much as anyone. It's cold
& enough that these phantom pains

rise up the telephone pole for a branch,
out the branch & for a leaf. When I bend
you're taller than I remember, than I
expected. We share the planet, a system

&, in its circling round the Milky Way,
there's no effect, no thick purpose
between the residue & fire. O Reader,
O Master, what do we do but try our luck

upon meeting a stairwell like vertebrae
ill-fitted, beyond repair. Tip my hat
& déjà vu in two hundred thirty million
years, be it carried or be the joyride

miraculous, yes, the cool spot of the moon
here passing the sun. Could've been us
swinging our might against the trees,
rather a narrow footing where the clouds

shrug with a density all their own. Evil
error in failing to imitate a calendar
pinned, my impulse to remove, sever,
withdraw from a tenure so antiseptically

massed (clobbered) & you'd be amazed too
what damage the single egg will wreak,
how much flesh a staple can pinch,
pop, swallow. The equivalent of a sigh

or a green sock missing in the machinery,
I quit late & walk the strand alone. We
skimmed the chapter baring sutures
& other methods. For what a body holds

no wonder we're drawn where the wave
scuttles & wears, & washes the stones
'til we say grains of sand. Supposing
spoilers & in the end everyone's rightly

famished, limb in a sling & to our liking
those who gaze, them whose dull manner
locks over supper with a priest. Easy
faith & whatnot to assume a celebration,

that a rough translating of the empty sleeve
might resuscitate for a common prayer,
reward a spectator like me. A month
slips speechless, repeatedly, then slams

back on her hinge for good. To avoid
what I've flopped while sweating this girl
well, gee whiz, be the kind of friend
who's quick to tender a bottle & agree

shit needs no reason. I was a quiet,
nominally adjusted tyke, nervous knees
knocking the table & the lesser loves
meowed at the bowl, greeted days

after days of sloppy drinking. Names,
where it happened, survey of the ancients
& their occasions done. I'm a coward,
tremulous, because guess who's here

& sudden, as if restored from a small burial
or nowhere weekend. Liquidy posture,
itching for the ocean & I a snail in tugging
your bandage clear. I cannot pretend

we'll make it outside of thought, a message
thumbed by my kitchen bulb. I say lay
but suppose a lie that pines for you & me,
points of reference, pink slip & so on

when the shine over a sweet, Ohio sky
submits, more soundly our country
bedims & cries one out. To be, to a truth
translucent, what else of such craving

besides a cotton square from a stranger,
cockcrow charged & for the record
my child pleads tooth & nail: no more,
no, no more school. Nevertheless

I've dug, & into its deep bargain a room
obliquely, doused, towering, & snuck
beneath a wallpaper some pumping thing
like foot traffic lost, the path muscled

& pitched, the bower upside down or bare,
shoulder to bare shoulder. Add to that
suppose for a yard all darkness melts
like clockwork, the proximity of a house

related to the stance of hydrants red
& bonnets white, the ignition churning
two towns away. To the last penny,
February insists on figures like a corpse

wrapped in wet cloth, a crayon silhouette
blowing the avenue. I've my wee ear
& a whim reversing winter from where
I write you with a lug nut & tire iron,

chawing straw, long past spooning
Amish honey before our hairline legs
almost curl into bed. Past the groundhog
where we found him or he finds us,

beginning with those how-do-you-dos
& floating in an outdoor pool. Reduced,
maybe some mornings we set forth
then mistake reflection more electric

than its source, the threshold crossed,
swerving (say yes) like a team of horses
shot loose & beyond. Then a wind chime,
then laughter, then out from hollows

your pattern for lucky weather. I whip
my jangle as though wild & split umbrellas
abound, our skin yet damp, hovering
lists of propositions, the a-e-l in Michael

& a speck of our father whistling us back
where frost now hikes the dunes. Yesterday
relieves the gull for a sparrow, regards
her host hunched over the table, this table

before, at last, taking leave. The hours
commence in gloaming, drop their shirts
& gallop the ebbing tide. They gather
driftwood & shells, negotiate the slow,

certain flame that collapses every starburst
like ash. Despite such fevers, suppose
you've welcomed my fondness for water
& into the future our various charms

form a fine collection. The offing says
melody slackens, even in luminosity
& ink, its what's what bidding farewells,
goodbye, yet the stream tells me otherwise.

Diamond Shoals

What a jolt, no polished stone nor summer
sleeping by the sea, but like a hinge
pointed loosely from its armor the late
& holy lance of a horseshoe finds her soft,
unsuspecting mark. Let the corollary show
flies like midair ember, a rabbit's grin
not unscathed between the dune & waterline
while the pebbly moon strikes to it
budding schoolboys peeling away bare,
wild with trembling, who give their dash
as if drunk on the heavens. Nearly
I'm quilled, nearly bliss in what's bled
yet onwardly bleeds. O lifeless fossil,
ghost of the unchristened soldier, surely
now you've met the deckhand & thief,
each risen then flattened again for your spear
lickety through the feet. Whatever stand
remains like nerve puts a finger there,
bears down, deep & crazed inside the sting
until not even the gods thick with clot
come calling, not even to the cusp
where they say the ocean eases terror,
washes smooth our sins like the eye
& thread as they mend, almost, this skin.

The Kissing Idiot

Sleep well, child, you're losing steam
& re-remember the fallen crest
when any cardinal quits the branch,
scatters the Sunday Savers as if erasing
this hamlet left yellow with waste.

Mercy shoots a feverish star (or two)
while the bone-dry, churchyard rubbing
splits, this age like each before,
exceptional as a Thanksgiving snooze.

Darling, such a down-to-earth lawn,
sheepish & whitewashing who bedded who
(or whom), what pissinlit hung seed,
smoked no little grass by the turtle pool
& since the weather says frost tonight
why not some tomfoolery more,
wet our teeth beneath the mulberries.

I took my tell-all by routine & the heart
where it wobbled unscrews, launches
like an arrow 'til its willful target
stutters, & slackens, then shits.

Pass here the gravy boat, & kindly deny
eyeing the flower when your decade
settles like dew, like better play it
cool around the sleeping grounds,
their airy, well-fed, ever-enormous trees.

On Learning of a Friend's Divorce

Even so, the dizzy months mean nothing,
slipshod in a rapidly binding, mundane
detail of the everyday & without thinking

for instance of palm trees, of the plenties
& how they converge, feverish when leaning
steep, clamorous before we each came

hardened to such weather. Twenty years
or twenty-five, off the stoop the easy quarter
rolls &, as after our shirt buttons pop,

swerves between a blindfold & that source
of what torrential light filters through,
blots the traffic color into a likeness

gone among the weeds. On similar dreams
another winter flops, bottoms what we
nowadays call a good marriage, moreover

belittles any ounce of comfort, recklessly
swept, the onlooker's mind astonished,
alone. It seems beneath our reason bending

mercy into a hull or against the thicket
housing January, where misgivings dwell,
to beg a second path as to sustain the parade

of snowy plovers, neutral birds who hurry
& skirt the salient backwash. This life
it gleams, dissolves like bitters or honey,

our footprints flush, rubbed clean with sand
& even so, in breathless velocity, the sky
reclines, tilting out of the clouds the moon

makes a pink balloon & then, by the burst
deckled & blazed, that rainbow more lavish
than a painting fastens her sails, awakens

how we once considered our shadows
like gods, colossal & able to bear the injury,
the lie, both a wrongdoing & its remedy

while the waves reply, heap their measures
of air or, given a chance, spur the hours
straightaway, split bright, no longer blind.

Mercy Killing

If only a dream, the selfsame dream
& now before mulling what's to be done
he obeys the rule, the must, ceding

by all means the dark conversion
more cloud than a blink, more mud
than flushing wing. I've made many men

bend a knee at the fence, whisper
as they would beside their dying fathers,
made of them a grove where the pine

disappears. Each levels his blade,
aims like a Lord who will not forgive
my make, what my life must answer for.

Bottled in Glass Where the Flavor Lasts

We repeat thank you & please, practice new letters of the week. We ready our crayons to circle Ms. Edmondson's glasses, looping from her collar the pale purple bow. We say Indian crisscrossing down to the rug. The various leaves stapled neatly, all the numbers we'll ever need &—beyond the high windows—cloud after cloud after cloud. We trace our hands at Thanksgiving, then count the rings, tear them one after one until there's no more red or green. By alphabet we march to the library, for the hour of music on Tuesdays. We lay our heads & warm breath across the tiny desks. We are cheddar sticks & juice from Dixies. We are dry-eyed when Joey Hawkins cries. Each morning our mothers leave us at the door.

Cricket Hill

Before its hour, flickering from another
year we've nearly failed to remember
but suddenly climb, childless again

between the girls & boys balancing
bright saucers or, presto, the improvised
box, way up the footpath for the snow

while in their cars on Lake Shore Drive
so many adults we imagine like loneliness
motor past, no feeling in their hands

& our fingers numb for the steep pleasure
absolved by the sled, hurrying each cry
that echoes its innermost joy when my hat

was yours & yours my lifeline, buried
where we dust our thighs, tender the glove
quick with I love you, knowing already

by clouds ghostly & fleeing our mouths,
amid the fugitive blur in a seemingly
clear & colossal air, how it must turn out.

If the Rule You Follow Leads You Here

On the branch the flamboyant, nosey forager
barely seen in these parts, flame off a wick
or else an American Redstart, rare, smaller

than an everyday sparrow in the season of May,
wings ignited. I know my share who will say
shopworn if tempting such a bird, overdone

despite how some landing patterns shift & mine
nearly a quieting but for my child's mouth
working apples like a windup toy. Oh in what

reason among others do I spin my own gears
insatiably, not the silver thrum when alone
& not the endless stutter like those weeks ago

when led to a ledge for poetry at the faraway
end of the register & below Fantasy. Listen,
my mind's an undertow in which our heels

catch behind the shed for parts, dragging dirt
for that lack of what is found when, for instance,
my child arrives to grind a green harmonica,

his calling blazed forward & hauling its freight
like a train, nothing short of a curious story
disrupted where speech resumes. I'm nodding,

open to the fires my bones have begun to fuel,
such frequencies even within the sentence
where I used to swim all afternoon, dwelling

in the what-I-wouldn't-gives & for one more
quarter hour slicing limes with my brother
gone, cheer each garnished glass to the brim,

revived & strong. Only so much light remains,
streams distance, common as overturning
filter & grounds before the new garbage liner

opens like a parachute & settles its tired form
for I suspect an imprecise simile as what's
precisely needed. I'm willing to try anything,

fabricate every Eastern Towhee, sparrows
indeed & red inside these summer miles south,
speed into sound, needing the running start,

steam or pep or pair of wings if I'm to finish
free enough of what surges, flinches & my aches
down the right leg. I'm asking for everything,

mercy me & the patient ear because I was told
no one sells that kind of book anymore, not
like they used to & I cave, crave the former day

to be some child trying not to crush the worms
flooding my way from their darkness. I look
again, this tendency familiar to many poets

& back to the beginning, branches & the birds,
oh my forthright birds, tell me when did you
sing last for the full sun above, fumble the grub,

its own hymn that can batten like a window
against the sudden breeze, reemerge & tremble,
delight in the instant, any instant, this instant.

The Afterlife

Having broken my vows with autumn,
every syllable for what feels like warmer
valley air. Having said my goodbyes

to wilderness, to dirt, to the childhood
slack on my face. Having gathered my share,
tailored chains out of clover & the apple

verily done. Having momently the heart
slip among the fettered boats. Having
delight not only in the queen but the honey

uncrowned. Having let my drowsy feet
commit to the flood song, the husband song,
song of the cockcrow & the headlong

regrets. Having indulged the late flowers,
delighted & moaned after the jukebox
took my riches whole. Having crooned,

having scorn, having then succumbed
to the world of waiting. Having made fires,
comraderies, asked & heard nothing

from the sea. Having prized the moon,
whimsical, whose bare & ample light
breezes through the hive, its murmuring

hushed. Having worshiped the untold lips,
skipped countless stones &, soothed
each time as the rippled surface mends,

now I must keep the promise of my body
to the bite, of my burrow for the snow,
& sleep beneath the green in the wild fields.

MICHAEL ROBINS is the author of four previous collections, including *In Memory of Brilliance & Value* and *People You May Know,* both from Saturnalia Books. He lives in the Portage Park neighborhood of Chicago.

....

Also by Michael Robins:

The Next Settlement
Ladies & Gentlemen
In Memory of Brilliance & Value
People You May Know

....

The Bright Invisible is printed in Baskerville.
www.saturnaliabooks.org